AHAB

The Real Authority behind Jezebel

Sandi Niven

Kingdom Publishers

AHAB
Copyright© Sandi Niven

All rights reserved. No part of this book may be reproduced in any form by photocopying or any electronic or mechanical means, including information storage or retrieval systems, without permission in writing from both the copyright owner and the publisher of the book. The right of Sandi Niven to be identified as the author of this work has been asserted by her in accordance with the Copyright, Designs and Patents Act 1988 and any subsequent amendments thereto.
A catalogue record for this book is available from the British Library.

All Scripture Quotations have been taken from the Amplified Version of the Bible.

ISBN: 978-1-913247-85-0

1st Edition by Kingdom Publishers
Kingdom Publishers
London, UK.

You can purchase copies of this book from any leading bookstore or email **contact@kingdompublishers.co.uk**

DEDICATION

To Linda Heidler – thank you so much for taking the time to read the first draft and a very special thanks for your valuable input. I pray this does it justice. A HUGE 'Thank You' to David and Valerie for making this possible. You have truly blessed me in ways I cannot repay! A final thanks to all my friends who have encouraged me and who have believed that I had books in me. You have challenged me and hopefully this is just the beginning.

CONTENTS

Prologue	9
Introduction	11
Chapter 1 *Ahab*	15
Chapter 2 *Ahab's Characteristics/Personality Traits*	19
Chapter 3 *Jezebel, Python and the Others*	29
Chapter 4 *Python / Divination*	32
Chapter 5 *The Others...*	36
Chapter 6 *The Journey*	37
Chapter 7 *The Knowledge*	39
Chapter 8 *So...have You Played Ahab to that Jezebel Spirit?*	41
Chapter 9 *Freedom!*	43
Chapter 10 *Divination Unwrapped*	47

Chapter 11 51
Principles

Chapter 12 55
The Helmet

Chapter 13 60
Testimony Time

Chapter 14 68
The Cleansing

Chapter 15 72
The Walk

Chapter 16 74
The Wrap Up

Characteristics list for easy Reference 75

PROLOGUE

Never has it been more important to expose the Ahab spirit than at 'such a time as this'. Whilst Ahab gives Jezebel authority, she will continue to hold open the door to Divination and every other demonic force the enemy can throw at us.

When the Lord recently spoke these words, "Divination is rife in the world today", I realised that writing this book was all the more urgent!

Divination **is** rife in the church and therefore rife in the world around us. Just watch the 'fake' news in all forms of the media.

Not only is the Church playing Ahab to that Jezebel spirit but so is the world and while we sit in ignorance the enemy gains ground.

The false prophets are fomenting violence and, while the church allows them the platform by playing Ahab to that spirit, it will only get worse!

Fake news has become the order of the day as newscasters and journalists lie with impunity! I liken them to the false prophets of Baal who 'divined' during the reign of Ahab and Jezebel.

It is time for the Church to wake up to the fact that she is intended to affect the world positively around her. Once she does, only then will things begin to change.

Sadly, we are the reason for the season!

The enemy will always overplay his hand by revealing, in a negative way, what God is wanting cleaned up. This needs to happen, firstly, in His Church in order that she, through prayer and anointed witnessing, can begin to affect society around her.

It's time for the true Elijahs to arise, to challenge these demonic forces and pull down the spiritual 'Baal' temples and altars in order for the world to see who The One True God is.

Whilst Ahab is firmly on the throne, with Jezebel at his side, ruling in his stead, this will not happen. And whilst Jezebel is ruling **legally**, she will continue to hold the door open to divination.

To have a greater understanding of the spirit of Jezebel we need to dig deeper to recognise, not only which spirits operate with her but **who gives her authority**. We need to know how to strip her of that authority, **individually** as well as **corporately**, and then to deal with her cohorts, as she certainly does not operate alone.

Once we have done this within the church, we will begin to effectively change society around us.

It is essential that we rightly discern, and then deal with, these demonic forces in order for the Body to survive the trying times ahead. My hope is that this book will be a tool in the hand of the reader to do just that.

Which brings me to the title of this book. I believe Ahab, the least spoken of character in the scheme of things, is the main culprit for the authority Jezebel has in the earth today. If we can expose this spirit, we can begin to effectively close the door to these pervasive forces of darkness which are shutting out the voice of God's true prophets and bringing divination into the Church and into the world today.

As this book is primarily written for the purpose of study, I would caution you to check the scriptures yourself. So, along with Paul, I exhort you, especially where I have only used references, to read the scriptures yourself – "study to show yourself approved"!

INTRODUCTION

It's time for Ahab to die!!

For years I have heard many teachings and have read many books on the subject of Jezebel. Some made sense but, although they blessed me, left me feeling something was missing.

Having also counselled for many years, I have often come across, and dealt with, the Jezebel spirit. And, just as often, I questioned why people never became totally free. No matter how much binding and loosing we did – how much "deliverance" ministry – some just never seem to be free of this spirit.

I call it "cropping grass". The lawn looks great once it's mowed, no weeds visible, but within a short period of time it needs doing again! Because the root is never dealt with!

The reason being, most teachings deal with a Jezebel spirit, but seldom does anyone address the **Ahab spirit,** the very spirit which I believe gives Jezebel authority. Neither do many of these teachings address the **spirit of divination - Python** - who is the fiend and strongman to whom the Jezebel spirit opens the door.

The first thing I need to clarify is that we are dealing with **spiritual characteristics, or traits, of demonic forces.** These are **neither male nor female.** In other words, just as the Jezebel spirit is not gender specific, neither are the Ahab, Python or any other spirits. I'll explain as I go along.

I will try to make this as practical, and as succinct as possible. Much is often lost in the use of more words than are necessary. And though I need to give some historical background to these characters, I do not want to emphasise the background, but bring more understanding of who we're dealing with.

Proverbs 4:5 *<u>Get</u> skillful and godly Wisdom, <u>get</u> understanding (discernment, comprehension, and interpretation); <u>do not forget and do not</u> turn back from the words of my mouth. (**Amp**) (underlining mine)*

I believe wisdom, knowledge and understanding give us greater authority.

Ephesians 6:12 *For we are not wrestling with flesh and blood [contending only with physical opponents], but against the despotisms, against the powers, against [the master spirits who are] the world rulers of this present darkness, against the spirit forces of wickedness in the heavenly (supernatural) sphere.*

Complacency has long been a huge problem within the Church and it wasn't until, some years back, after much reading and study, that I began to understand who the spirit behind this complacency truly is.

Due to previous incomplete and sometimes even incorrect teachings we are, as the Church, inclined to be pretty blinkered in our understanding of certain truths. We've yet to have all leaders teach the FULL Gospel in our pulpits! Much of this comes through the lack of **personal** understanding of the Word. A commodity - for lack of a better word - sadly lacking in many in the Church.

We have become too reliant on a handful of men and women seeking revelation from God, while the rest sit on their "seats of learning" (rear ends) and do nothing. For too long the Saints have been 'taught at' instead of equipped. Then, because we all only hear in part and see in part, we only receive one or two facets of the truth, instead of seeking the Lord <u>individually</u> to receive more than just the portions of revelation brought from the pulpits.

My hope and aim in writing this book, is to bring a greater awareness to the Body of the danger we face if these spirits are not dealt with soon, and correctly. My hope too, is that this will stir you personally to seek the Lord for deeper revelation and knowledge. He is pouring out so much at this time because of the *Kairos* (God's opportune time) and *Kainos* (new and fresh) times we're in, that it would be a shame for anyone to miss out.
Remember you are in this world, right now, for a purpose!

This is not a book of methodology! We've been so caught up in the "how" that we forget we have an Almighty God who "changes not" yet is constantly changing!! If you don't understand that then you don't understand God! *The true sons of God are **led** by the Spirit of God.* Time for us to stop just quoting that scripture but to start walking in it!

Many who will read this book will immediately think of someone else they know to whom much will apply. But it is time for us to be honest and examine our ***own*** hearts and motives and to clean our ***own*** hands **first**, in preparation for the onslaught ahead of us. Allow Holy Spirit to bring revelation to you as you read and ask Him to show you where you need to deal with issues in your own life. Deal with them and put them in the past where they belong so that we can move forward to what God has in the future for us. Only once you've dealt with your own heart can you begin to effectively pray for others!

So, let us pray first:

> *Lord Jesus, I thank You that You are Lord over my life and that the blood of Jesus covers me as a child of the Most High God. I ask Holy Spirit of God that You will come alongside me as I study this material and bring revelation. Your word says to call for understanding and I call for it now. I also ask for wisdom which*

*You promise to give in abundance. Your word says that **knowing** the truth will set me free. My desire is to be free of any and all of the influences of the enemy and, as understanding comes, help me to apply Your wisdom and truth. I am trusting that You will reveal the lies of the enemy, that I may be totally set free in Jesus name. Amen*

Chapter 1

Ahab

It took Ahab, of the Book of Kings, to give Jezebel a throne. He married her, gave her a throne and thereby "relegated" authority to her. It was not an automatic ruling in that day that the King's wife became Queen. In fact, women did not usually have much say in those times and many kings had several wives, as did Ahab. What is interesting is that Jezebel was the only one of his wives who wielded authority.

So, why do we only teach or preach about Jezebel? As I began to see it, if there was no Ahab then there could be no Jezebel.

HOW CAN JEZEBEL HAVE AUTHORITY IF THERE IS NO AHAB TO GIVE HER AUTHORITY?

We need to see all of these spirits for who they are in reality. Each has different characteristics but, at the end of the day, they all have one purpose – to shut the mouths of the prophets.

Who is he?

Ahab's name means "brother, or friend of his father." That in itself shows something of his origins.

He was the son of, and successor to, Omri and was the seventh king of Israel's Northern Kingdom. He married Jezebel, as part of a trade agreement with the Sidonian king. Scripture tells us he incited God's anger more than any of Israel's previous kings. He reigned for 22 years, much of which was marred by spiritual compromise and failure (**1 Kings 16:30**).

Under Ahab's rule there was a tremendous growth of wealth but at the expense of serious spiritual apostasy.

1 Kings 22:39, as well as various other historical references, tells us Ahab built an ivory palace for Jezebel. According to historians, the rooms and furniture, in many cases, featured Egyptian deities.

1 Kings 16:31 – 33 tells us that Ahab began bowing in worship to Baal after he married Jezebel. He then built a temple and an altar to Baal in Samaria, after which he set up an Ashtoreth (Phoenician goddess of love and increase).

Baal worship was a Pagan religion which pursued Child-sacrifice and every kind of perversion. Their Temples housed prostitutes, male and female and their so called priests were known for their 'divining' – false prophecy.

Ahab *appears* to have been a worshiper of God as well, but most definitely along with other deities. He was a compromiser yet consulted with God's prophets (**1 Kings 20:13-14,22,28; 22:8,16**). His "compromising" attributes are well reflected in the fact he did not interfere with the execution of God's prophets by Jezebel or even the execution of Jezebel's false prophets after the contest on Mt. Carmel (**1 Kings 18:40**).

The influence of Jezebel in his life overshadowed any significant influence the prophets of the Lord had in his life. He became a prime example of evil according to **Micah 6:16** *For the statutes of [idolatrous] Omri you have kept, and all the works of the house of [wicked] Ahab, and you walk in their counsels....* (I suggest you read the full chapter)

Our first encounter with Ahab

1Kings 16:25-33

To put it politely, he did not have the best of fathers. His father **Omri** *"did evil in the eyes of the Lord, even worse than all who were before him."* (**vs 25**) By the way, the name Omri has the connotation of one who *'piles on blows'* – which sounds pretty much like a bully to me!

Verse 30 tells us that Ahab continued the trend and *"did evil in the sight of the Lord above all before him."* So, he was in fact worse than his father.

Verse 31 – (***my paraphrase***) *If that wasn't enough, he then took a foreigner for a wife, a Baal priestess at that, and he served Baal and worshipped him.*

Verse 33 - *Ahab did more to provoke the Lord, the God of Israel, to anger than all the kings of Israel before him.*

That's some legacy!

Then Elijah comes on the scene. **1Kings 17:1**.

An interesting fact is, because Ahab was king, and even though he did wrong in the sight of the Lord, Elijah was not given authority by God to "slay" him. I believe Elijah honoured the position of "king" which Ahab held, even though he knew Ahab was doing evil in the sight of the Lord. Just as David had honoured Saul and refused to kill him. Both certainly had the opportunity to do so.

It was not Elijah's place to judge or deal with Ahab's sin. As Prophet, he could speak as the Lord directed him and show the people of Israel their error, but Ahab's life itself was God's to deal with. A lesson we in the Body would do well to emulate when it comes to our leaders!

IT WAS NOT ELIJAH'S PLACE TO JUDGE OR DEAL WITH AHAB'S SIN

Elijah did, however, deal with Baal worship and got rid of the false prophets. God Himself would deal with Ahab later.

As we see in **1 Kings 22,** Ahab eventually put **himself** in a position where he could be taken out by the enemy. It's well worth the read and certainly well worth the warning regarding ignoring or disdaining God's true prophets!

Read 1 Kings, chapters 19 – 22 I will refer to them further along.

Chapter 2

Ahab's Characteristics / Personality Traits

To understand how the Ahab spirit opens the door to Jezebel and her cohorts we need to look at what constitutes an Ahab-type personality. This means we need to look at Ahab, the person, to see who we're dealing with. What is it about him that gives Jezebel authority?

Once I understood that this Ahab spirit, or personality type, was the open door which gave Jezebel authority and power, things became a whole lot clearer.

Instead of closing the door to the one who relegates or even delegates that authority, we have focussed on the Jezebel spirit and left the door of access wide open. This, I believe, is the reason we've been so ineffective in dealing with the spirit of Jezebel and, as we will later see, the spirit of divination.

RELEGATE (vb) - *to transfer, entrust, assign, commit, or to deputise.*

So, in order to close this door, we need to know what actually constitutes an Ahab-type personality. As we study who and what Ahab did, in scripture, we are better able to discern these characteristics. Firstly, in ourselves and then in others. **Not for judgement of others** but, hopefully, in order to set us all free.

There is some serious repentance necessary in the Body!

What then constitutes an Ahab personality?

Ahab was an arrogant man and, obviously, wielded very little authority in his own house. Jezebel ruled the roost. She slew the prophets of God and Ahab stood by and did nothing. Yes, she was a strong character, but Ahab was king. He had the power and authority to prevent her from having any say at all, yet he chose to bow to her authority.

Because of the arrogance in Ahab's heart, the belief that he could do no wrong, or even be held accountable for any wrongdoing, opened the door for Jezebel to take, and have, more authority that she should. I believe he also sees her as being 'spiritually' more mature than him because of her connection to Baal worship. This will become more evident as we go along.

1 Kings chapters 20 and 21 give huge insight into Ahab's character. Watch how the various scenes in these Chapters play out.

1Kings 20:1 - 12

Ben-Hadad, king of Syria, gathers thirty-two other kings and besieges Samaria. He sends messengers to Ahab telling him that he is going to take Ahab's wives and children captive. Ahab doesn't even fight back. He immediately backs down, doesn't even argue with Ben-Hadad; he says – Sure, take everything! I'll even deliver them to you!

He is arrogant and doesn't handle conflict well, so always takes the line of least resistance.

Ben-Hadad responds by saying he now wants all Ahab's silver and gold as well as his family, and tells Ahab he will send his own servants to search the houses and make sure Ahab holds nothing back.

Only then does Ahab go to his elders to complain that Ben-Hadad is threatening him <u>personally</u>. **My** wives, **My** children, **My** silver and **My** gold! Forget the fact the whole of Israel is being besieged! Every threat or attack, with Ahab, is perceived to be personal, with little or no consideration for the people he serves. He portrays a martyr complex –

believes everyone to be against him. This makes him selfish and self-serving.

When his elders, and the people, tell him not to respond to Ben-Hadad (**vs8**), he shows his disdain for their counsel and basically ignores them. He is a law unto himself.

Then what amazed me was how he compromised. He sends a message back to Ben-Hadad telling him he can still have the wives, children, silver and gold – what he's already promised – but tells Ben-Hadad he can't send his servants in! (**vs9**)

I just bet his wives and children must have thought very highly of him!

Fortunately for Israel, God intervenes and routs the enemy. But the Prophet then warns Ahab, (**vs 22**). He says *"Go, fortify yourself and become strong and give attention to what you must do, for at the first of next year the king of Syria will return against you."* Ahab doesn't heed the warning and because of it becomes even more deceived. He disobeys God and ends up making covenant with his enemy!

After the Prophet confronts Ahab with his disobedience and lack of discernment. He tells Ahab, **vs42**, *"Thus says the Lord: Because you have let go out of your hand the man I had devoted to destruction* (meaning Ben Hadad whom Ahab had made covenant with), *therefore your life shall go for his life, and your people for his people."* (Brackets mine)

Vs 43 Ahab becomes resentful and sullen. He hates correction. He doesn't easily take advice and sees any form of correction as personal criticism.

His insecurity makes him easily manipulated and causes him to relegate even more authority to Jezebel. It also diverts the responsibility and accountability away from him. It's always someone else's fault!

Ahab is a whiner and can appear petulant and greedy. The perfect example of his petulance and greed is seen in the account of Naboth's vineyard.

1 Kings 21:1 – 16

Ahab approaches Naboth, demands he give him his vineyard. Naboth refuses and tells Ahab the <u>legal</u> reason why he won't, or rather can't, give the vineyard to Ahab – **vs3** – *"The Lord forbid that I should give the inheritance of my fathers to you."*

Ahab has absolutely no regard for God's laws. Had he gone about it the right way, and if Naboth had been willing, he could have purchased the property for a length of time (50 years) – per the property laws set in **Leviticus 25:14 - 16.**

God had ordained that property was man's inheritance and therefore could not be sold. He does, however, allow the people to sell a property, if the owner is willing, for a period of 50 years. In today's language this would amount to a 50-year leasehold. After which the property would revert back to the natural owner. But Ahab believes he's entitled and as a result throws a hissy fit! He sulks!

Vs 4 *And Ahab, already depressed by the Lord's message to him (***1Kings 20:42** *– related above) came into his house <u>more resentful and sullen</u> because of what Naboth the Jezreelite had said to him; for he had said, I will not give you the inheritance of my fathers. And he lay down on his bed, turned away his face, and would eat no food.* (brackets and underline mine)

He is resentful, sullen and sulks when he doesn't get his own way. He also sulks when people aren't paying attention to him, or people oppose him.

Look then too at how his whining and complaining empower Jezebel and allow her to step in and take control.

Vs7 *Jezebel his wife said to him, Do you not govern Israel?* (Aren't you the leader?) *Arise, eat food and let your heart be happy. <u>I will give</u> you the vineyard of Naboth the Jezreelite.* (Bracket and underline mine)

Jezebel uses her relegated authority to write letters in Ahab's name and begins discrediting Naboth. The long and the short of it is that Naboth is eventually removed (murdered) because of false accusations or testimonies set against him by Jezebel. Problem solved! **(vs8 – 14)** Jezebel hands over Naboth's vineyard to Ahab.

Note that Naboth's family also had no say! But God always justifies!!

The Lord then speaks to Elijah and sends him to confront Ahab, down in Naboth's vineyard. Have a look at his disdain for God's prophet. **Vs20** *Ahab said to Elijah, Have you found me, O my enemy?*

Elijah's response is interesting. *"I have found you, because you have sold yourself to do evil in the sight of the Lord."*

Disobedience (sin) causes us to trade with God's glory. Instead of God being the focus and receiving the glory in our lives, we then become the focus. God will share His glory with no man!

Elijah then prophesies both Ahab and Jezebel's demise.

1Kings 21:21 – 26
See says the Lord, I will bring evil on you and utterly sweep away and cut off from Ahab every male, bond and free. And will make your household like that of Jeroboam son of Nebar and like the household of Baasha son of Ahijah, for the provocation with which you have provoked Me to anger and made Israel to sin. Also, the Lord said of Jezebel: The dogs shall eat Jezebel by the wall of Jezreel. Any belonging to Ahab who dies in the city the dogs shall eat, and any who dies in the field the birds of the air shall eat. For there was no one who sold himself to do evil in the sight of the Lord as did Ahab, incited by his wife Jezebel. He did very abominably in going after idols, as had the Amorites, whom the Lord cast out before the Israelites. (Underline mine)

Ahab's reaction was interesting **(vs27)**. He actually repents. The Lord relents and says He will not bring about the destruction of Ahab's house in his lifetime but rather in the next generation. God will always justify.

A side note here. What caught my eye in the prophecy is, the Lord says He will *cut off every male, bond or free*. This might seem harsh but the influence Ahab has over the people who 'serve' him will corrupt down through the generations. It becomes a generational curse which will always rear its head later unless dealt with appropriately.

Unfortunately for Ahab, his repentance doesn't last long. His lack of the fear of God, as well as his disdain for God's prophets, causes all the other characteristics to raise their heads once again, and more so.

Ahab not only lacks discernment but is disobedient to the voice of the Lord. He is primarily a "hearer" of the word of the Lord but seldom a "doer" – which, by the way, the word calls deception (**James 1:22**).

He is obedient only when it suits him. He is a "do as I say" type of person who very seldom actually practices what he preaches and is controlled, pretty much, by a religious spirit. He is often the type of person Jeremiah says has God "*near their mouths but far from their hearts*". (**Jeremiah 12:2**) One who will talk a good talk, say all the right things and use scripture to cover the emptiness in his heart.

As we have seen in these accounts in **1Kings 20 and 21**, Ahab, because of "pride of position," is unteachable and will constantly try to justify his standpoint. He demands respect for his position – immaterial of whether he has earned it or not – and doesn't give proper honour where honour is due, because of his self-focus and a lack of understanding of true honour. This is all evident in his dealings with Elijah, his elders and others.

He is also covetous – as we have seen in his dealings with Naboth (**1Kings 21**)

If the prophets don't prophesy what he wants – what would tickle his ears or make him look good – he doesn't want to hear them. I call this "entertainment prophecy".

A further example of his inattention to, and disdain of, prophets is seen in the following.

1 Kings 22:9-27 Micaiah the prophet warns Ahab about going into battle. He tells him that a lying spirit has been sent by God to entice him into battle. But because it doesn't suit Ahab's plans, he ignores the Prophet. The word doesn't make him look good in front of the other kings, and as a result, he has the prophet imprisoned and ignores the warning. To his downfall, of course! You can read the account yourselves.

Please understand! A person controlled by an Ahab spirit does not have to portray ALL of these characteristics! **One or two will be enough to empower Jezebel.**

Definitions

Let us unpack some of these characteristics or personality traits in order to make them more identifiable – perhaps even in our own lives.

A whiner – someone who whinges like a child when they don't get their own way. Sulky and petulant.

Covetous – we all know what greed is but this is more. This is inordinately desiring what's not yours – what belongs to someone else – because you feel you're more entitled than them to have it. One of the 10 commandments of what **not** to do!

This also applies to coveting ministries the Lord has not commissioned or called you to! Trying to emulate other ministries when you do not have the call or commission of God will lead you to deceive those around you.

Non-confrontational - seeing problems and not addressing them – in the hope they will just go away, or hoping that perhaps someone else will deal with them. What I would term an "ostrich" mentality – head in sand!

Confrontation is not always a negative but be careful that it doesn't swing the other way, where confrontation becomes just another excuse for an argument! Confrontation should never be avoided, but it's the attitude of heart when confronting that must always be kept in mind.

Taking the line of least resistance - trying to please everyone whether they are right or not. Pretty much the same as the characteristic above. Scared of rocking the boat. Making excuses for why things are the way they are. Avoiding confrontation, however, will empower Jezebel and give her free reign.

Controlling - (this is linked with **pride**) likes having his/her own way. My way or the highway! Also, one who micro-manages instead of trusting those he has oversight of. Perverted authority. When you operate in true God given authority Holy Spirit will be in total control and you will know it – so will everyone else.

Unteachable - Something we would all like to believe we are not but, has anyone ever tried to bring correction to you in any form? If you refuse to even consider that you might be wrong, then I believe you are showing signs of being unteachable. If you constantly feel the need to justify your standpoint, then you are definitely in trouble! God is your justifier not you! Teachability comes through humility.

Believing you're invulnerable to deception – that's just arrogance gone to seed! We are all susceptible to deception – hence the spiritual gift of discernment! Arrogance, however, will definitely make you feel invulnerable.

Pride of position - It is not the position, nor the title, which makes the man. Respect is earned not commanded – no matter who you are – king, leader or elder. God's appointments are not about a "title" but a "mantle" (a covering) which carries a God-given authority, and which is evident in the person's calling. Whatever "position" you **think** you have, if it doesn't "**humbly serve**" then it is merely a title. When people recognise your God-given authority then they will automatically respect and honour you. It's not because of who you are, but because of **who He is**! God appoints leaders and can just as easily dethrone them!

Self-centredness – Insecurity will foster the desire for constant affirmation and will cause this person to draw others around them who will pander to their every need and always be in agreement with them – whether right or wrong. "Yes" men/women!

Blame shifting – it is always someone else's fault. Again, the need to justify.

As I said, many of these characteristics will not always be immediately identifiable. They aren't always that blatant either and will often manifest in different combinations of ways. **Oftentimes they are underlying and don't always manifest till Jezebel makes her appearance.**

Those who are **arrogant and prideful** will be especially vulnerable to this spirit and will, without fail, enable Jezebel and her cohorts. It just takes "one" to open the door.

Some of the characteristics might seem a contradiction but all come out of a deep-seated insecurity. When we know who we are in Christ and walk humbly in this knowledge, we become more and more secure in ourselves and are able to walk in a righteous authority in Christ.

Yes, I know we can all think of someone else to whom one or more of the characteristics apply! **BUT this is not about them** – this is about you and me. When you point a finger, remember there are three fingers pointing back at you, so deal with yourself first!

IT JUST TAKES ONE TO OPEN THE DOOR!

Remember **Matthew 7:1** – Jesus says, *Do not judge and criticize and condemn others, so that you may not be judged and criticized and condemned yourselves. For just as you judge and criticize and condemn others, you will be judged and criticized and condemned, in accordance with the measure you [use to] deal out to others, it will be dealt out again to you.*

Funny thing is, Jezebel portrays many of these very same characteristics and therein lies the problem. Most people get blind-sided by her because they don't recognise these characteristics in themselves.

It's almost as though Ahab and Jezebel were cut from the same cloth. They both had selfish ambitions which aspired to more than the Lord had ordained for them and, because of that, felt they were above reproach.

The "gruesome twosome"! And then some....

I truly believe that Jezebel can only make an entrance when we're in disobedience or in rebellion. When we are not obeying God's word or His principles in any form, the enemy will always gain a foothold.

1Samuel 15:22b,23a Samuel speaking.. *Behold, to obey is better than sacrifice, and to hearken than the fat of rams. For rebellion is as the sin of witchcraft, and stubbornness is as idolatry and teraphim (household good luck charms).*

The Lord ties rebellion to rejection of His word!

REMEMBER THESE SPIRITS ARE NOT GENDER SPECIFIC AND CAN INFLUENCE, OR WORK, IN OR THROUGH, MALE AND FEMALE ALIKE.

Chapter 3

Jezebel, Python and the others...

As I said previously, much has been written about Jezebel and, because of that, I will try not go into too much detail. I am merely giving her background and noting her characteristics here for easy reference.

The main aim of this book is to expose the *spirit of Ahab* and see how he opens the door to Jezebel and her cohorts; Python (Divination), the Beguiling, Seducing and Controlling spirits.

Jezebel

Her name means, "Where is the prince?" perhaps derived from Phoenician name meaning, "Baal is the prince."

Other translations of her name are; "Baal exalts" or "Baal is husband to" or "Unchaste". These names all speak for themselves.

Like Ahab, she makes her entrance in **1 Kings 16** and, as the wife of Ahab, was an impious and cruel queen who introduced and protected idolatry, then persecuted and killed God's prophets.

She continued her evil influence through her son Joram (**2 Kings 9:22**). And her name has become so associated with wickedness that even the false prophetess in the church at Thyatira was thus labelled. (**Rev. 2:20**).

Elijah, although he never dealt personally with her, challenged her false prophets at Mt Carmel and slew them. This evoked Jezebel's threat to kill him (**1 Kings 19:2**) and he ran for his life.

What fascinated me was, nowhere in scripture does it mention Elijah ever openly confronting Jezebel. Even when he received the threatening note from her, he still did not confront her. In fact, he ran from her, which was surprising until I understood why. But we'll look at that a little later.

In the book of Revelation, however, the Lord, in His letter to the church at Thyatira (**Rev 2:20**) says *"But I have this against you: that you <u>tolerate</u> the woman Jezebel, who calls herself a prophetess [claiming to be inspired], and who is teaching and leading astray my servants and beguiling them into practicing sexual vice and eating food sacrificed to idols."* (underlining mine)

TOLERATE (vb) – *allow the existence, occurrence or practice of (something that one dislikes or disagrees with) without interference.*

This is a warning we cannot afford to ignore!

See how the beguiling and seducing spirits operate with her?

There is so much to unpack in this verse. Even though the Lord specifically addresses the church in Thyatira, I believe He is confronting this in us, as individuals, and more pertinently, those in leadership in the church today. The reason the deception is in the church, is because of the "Ahabs" in leadership. This is what is giving Jezebel a throne.

Jezebel's Characteristics / Personality Traits

As a high priestess of Baal, she was an idolater, a wicked seducer, a persecutor of the prophets of the Lord, and a great patroness of idolaters and false prophets. These were all tenets of Baal worship.

Jezebel is described as, subtle of heart; the mistress of manipulation, and knowing how, to serve her own base purposes.

She is loud and stubborn, self-willed, noisy and troublesome, willful and headstrong, all mouth, and will have her say, right or wrong. She is impatient of checks and controls, and cannot bear to be counseled, much less reproved.

REMEMBER, ALTHOUGH, FOR EASE OF WRITING, I SOMETIMES REFER TO THIS SPIRIT IN THE "FEMALE", THIS IS A SPIRIT AND DEFINITELY NOT GENDER SPECIFIC.

We saw in the account of Naboth's vineyard, how Jezebel ignored checks and controls. She will manipulate situations to take what she wants, in spite of the consequences, because she sees herself as above the law.

The Jezebel spirit always attracts attention to itself. It will use manipulation and control to keep the focus on itself rather than on the Lord. This has a lot to do with the Beguiling, Seducing and Controlling spirits who work hand in hand with this spirit.

This spirit gains entrance by making you think it has your best interests at heart. Will "minister" to you to gain favour – gain entrance – then will subtly begin to turn and assert its own authority. Its aim is to take your focus off the Lord. Because of a lack of discernment, it is often not recognized.

As I said previously, many of these characteristics are also found in Ahab, although maybe not as easily identifiable. They are almost like two sides of the same coin. They seem to have the same intent but portray the characteristics in different ways.

Chapter 4

Python / Divination

So, on we go with the domino effect.

Ahab initially opens the door to Jezebel, she in turn opens the door to the spirits of divination, a seducing spirit, a beguiling spirit and a controlling spirit.

I believe Jezebel, as evil as she is, does not actually do the work herself. She would see it as beneath her. She delegates by opening the door to these cohorts, all of whom are extremely effective in shutting down the prophetic voice. As we study them you will understand why.

Python, a snake of some renown!

Many have asked me about Divination through the years and I've been astounded at how few leaders know anything about this spirit or how it operates. Mind you, it took for the Lord to put certain books into my hands, to give me a lot more insight.

Why Python? You will see from the following how the association was derived.

Puthon (4436) from the Greek (**Poo'-thone**) from **Putho** the name of a region where Delphi, the seat of the famous oracle, was located. A Python, i.e. (by analogy with the supposed diviner there) inspiration (soothsaying): - **divination**. (Strong's Concordance)

Puthon **(python)** is connected with the cult of Apollo in ancient Greece. In Greek Mythology, Python was the serpent who guarded the oracle of

Delphi. This serpent was slain by Apollo, who then took on the name Apollo Pythias. Which, I believe, is where the occult brotherhood, Knights of Pythias are derived as well.

Diviners and soothsayers of old were associated with the cult of Apollo, and therefore operated in a ***spirit of python***.

Paul comes across this spirit in Philippi. ***Acts 16:16-18***. This is the story of the young slave girl who followed Paul and his team around – *shouting loudly, These men are the servants of the Most High God! They announce to you the way of salvation. And she did this for many days. Then Paul, being sorely annoyed and worn out, turned and said to the spirit in her, I charge you in the name of Jesus Christ to come out of her! And it came out that very moment.*

This seems to be the only reference to the actual **spirit of divination** in the New Testament.

Python's Characteristics

In the natural, a Python is one of the constrictor family of snakes. Back in Africa – where I'm from - they often will drop out of trees onto, and wrap themselves around, the unsuspecting victim. Another method is to slide up alongside their intended victim while it sleeps. It will measure itself, lengthwise against its victim to see if it – the snake – is long enough to swallow the victim. It then wraps around, and holds, its victim but does not immediately start squeezing or constricting. It waits until the victim exhales then tightens its hold and takes up that space, making it very difficult to inhale and fill the chest cavity again. This is how it slowly but surely suffocates its prey to death. Only then does it crush the victim and swallow it whole. It is a very slow process!

The python spirit, or spirit of divination manifests itself in much the same way. Its main aim is to "suffocate" or go after the "breath" of the prophets, **but it does not limit itself to the prophetic**. It will also choke out **any** vision or creativity.

It is an anti-Christ spirit!

What constitutes divination then? Go back to **Acts 16.** What the slave girl was shouting was actually the truth. Paul and Silas were servants of the Most High God. They were announcing the way of salvation. What gives away the fact that what the slave girl was saying was divination, is that Paul was *sorely annoyed and worn out.* God's truth will always refresh you but a truth revealed through divination will wear you down. It will take the focus off the Lord and put it on 'man'.

I should imagine the people who were listening to Paul and his team would have been 'impressed' with the slave girl 'knowing' these were men of God. The more she shouted though, the more the attention would have gone to her, rather than to what Paul and his team were ministering to the people.

This spirit is territorial and does not want believers to take a city or a nation. It makes people dependent on a particular group or leader for existence, taking away their ability to think or act of their own accord. It promotes co-dependency rather than inter-dependency. It draws man's attention away from God to other human beings and will cause people to undermine authority because of that.

Let us look at a few more characteristics of divination:

Love of money and fear of the loss thereof. We see this as the result of the spirit of divination being cast out of the slave girl. Her 'handlers' could no longer manipulate money from the people by her socalled 'knowledge'. So much so, that they accuse Paul and Silas of throwing the city into confusion! (**Acts 16:19 – 22**) The people had become so 'distracted' and focussed on the slave girl they joined her owners in beating Paul and Silas and eventually having them thrown in jail.

This spirit uses **diversionary tactics** – keeps you preoccupied or focussed in one area so it can have an opening in another; **causes confusion, unrest and fear**.

It also **manifests itself in apathy or lethargy,** often causing people to want to sleep during the church service or when reading the Word. I believe this is because it works so closely with a beguiling spirit which **lulls the people into a false sense of security**.

Note how similar the intent in these characteristics are to those of Ahab and Jezebel. Literally a case of "birds of a feather flock together"!

Once the spirit of Divination has entrance, it becomes the ruling spirit and the others then follow its lead and work alongside it to effectively stop ministry or block vision.

Recently I was sharing some of these truths with a friend in ministry and I likened the python spirit to the python, Ka, in Jungle Book. The picture is of Mowgli seduced/enticed to swing on a swing which Ka makes with his own body. Mowgli's eyes begin these spiralling circles as he looks into Ka's eyes and he is lulled into a false sense of security by the beguiling spirit. Python does the rest.

Chapter 5

The others...

Oftentimes, the reason we are not free of the spirit of Jezebel, or Ahab for that matter, is because we never deal with their cohorts. Because we have dealt with the main characters, does not mean we've defeated their cohorts as well!

Ahab opens the door to Jezebel; she in turn opens the door to Python (Divination) and the other spirits; Beguiling, Seducing and Controlling spirits.

Let us have a look at Dictionary definitions of these characteristics.

To Beguile.... means to *charm, attract, enchant or en-trance. To captivate, bewitch, spellbind, blind, hypnotize, mesmerize, deceive, mislead,* and so on. I think those words in themselves give us a pretty good picture.

To Seduce.... means to *attract, allure, tempt, cajole, wheedle, ensnare, charm, enchant, deceive, dupe.* It's interesting how similar this word is to beguile. It is also a word often used to express sexual 'charm'.

To Control.... this is pretty self-explanatory, especially in the negative sense of the word. It defines a person who *micro-manages; who holds the reins, refuses to, or has a hard time delegating. One who determines the behaviour of others. One who dominates; seeks more attention than usual; blame-shifts if things don't go right.*

It is important to remember, the reason that dealing with Ahab is the key to dealing with Jezebel, is that he portrays at least one, or more, of these characteristics as well. This shows me that they are already present and are just waiting for the door to open to be able to operate more freely within a wider spectrum.

Chapter 6

The Journey

Now that we've identified the characteristics of these demonic forces, let me share how I came to understand what I do about these principalities and powers. And I don't by any means have it all!!

Quite early on in ministry, Holy Spirit began opening my eyes to the effects of the spirit of Jezebel. We need to guard against it at all times, but recognising the spirit and knowing how to deal with it are key.

Being in prophetic ministry is never easy. There are always challenges which will attempt to wear you down and cause you to let your guard drop. I, however, had inadvertently gone into ministry with someone whom Jezebel used to undermine what God was doing through me. It took me a while to break free and God used two trusted Prophets, whom I'd known for several years, to speak very strongly into my life. I repented quickly and broke contact with this person.

Not long after I broke contact, I began really battling spiritually. Warfare not only increased but I, seemingly, was making no headway, or getting breakthrough. I sought counsel and the Lord led me to study the spirit of Jezebel in more depth, which led to a study on the spirit of Divination (Python) as well. I studied these for some time.

The prophetic had begun drying up in my life and I couldn't understand why. I would receive a word of prophecy from the Lord but thoughts would bombard my mind and tell me that the person I was ministering to wasn't really that interested to hear what "I" had to say or the words would simply 'evaporate' and I'd go blank. It had become more and more evident that I was battling a demonic force and knew it had something to do with the spirit of Jezebel. It just seemed too difficult or too much hassle to fight. I was constantly tired and I knew this shouldn't be. Everything I did was an effort and I felt the life was being squeezed out of me.

I understood the main focus of the Jezebel spirit had always been to shut the prophets up, but it seemed everything I did was to no avail. I'd read all the books, done all the usual - rebuked it and bound it - but nothing was working so I knew there was something deeper which I needed to understand.

What I didn't recognise till after much counsel was, instead of this being a random attack or because I was a commissioned prophet, **I had personally opened the door**. It began with insecurity and was furthered later by pride, in that I was too embarrassed to speak to anyone about what I was battling, in case they would think less of me.

In ignorance, or arrogance, I had believed I could "handle" what I had identified as a spirit of Jezebel operating against me, through the person I had been in ministry with, but I had never actually dealt with it. So, in effect I had opened the door to this attack by playing "Ahab" to that spirit. I had relegated it authority and it almost destroyed me and my ministry.

Because I didn't have the revelation I do now, that Ahab is the authority behind Jezebel, I continued to try and deal with Jezebel as I had in the past. That spirit, however, was not budging and things got worse. I still did not recognise that I was the problem. I had inadvertently – through lack of understanding, lack of discernment, as well as a host of other things – opened myself to an Ahab spirit. Until I repented and dealt with my own heart, I wasn't able to see clearly enough to deal with Jezebel or her cohorts.

I WAS THE PROBLEM!

Once I understood that I had opened the door myself and repented, I began binding Jezebel, once again to no avail. Holy Spirit once again came to the rescue! Because I was still missing something, I began asking specific questions of the Lord. This began a journey for me, the end result of which was deliverance and material for this book.

Chapter 7

The Knowledge

Whilst on a much-needed retreat, out of the blue, Holy Spirit asked me *"What is a eunuch?"* I was reading a novel at the time, so this was quite a surprise. I put down my book and thought about the question very carefully, because I knew He was asking for a reason. After reasoning it out, my answer, eventually, was *"someone who has been cut off from being fruitful"*.

A eunuch is one whose reproductive organs have been removed and therefore is unable to reproduce – hence "cut off from being fruitful". Makes sense doesn't it. Well actually that was a huge revelation.

Holy Spirit then asked *"Who killed Jezebel?"* Because I didn't want to make a mistake, I went to check it out and found it was the eunuch's who had thrown her down from the window, at Jehu's feet, where his horse and chariot then trampled her.

2 Kings 9:30 – 37 gives the account. The following is my paraphrase of the events.

Jezebel hears that Jehu is coming, assumes it is to see her, so dresses herself up to entice or seduce him. She sits in the window and calls down to him. Jehu, who is a type of the Lord Jesus, basically ignores her and calls out - "Who is on my side?". Two or three Eunuchs look out the window at him. He says *"throw Jezebel down"* so they do. She has rather a gory end, but Elijah had prophesied her death and it came to pass as he had said.

In this, Holy Spirit showed me how Jezebel was to be dealt with. Besides confronting my own heart, there was a principle I needed to heed and apply in order to see her demise in my life and ministry.

Interesting that she was sitting in the window, as windows represent the Prophetic. In other words, she is sitting in a lofty or a high place (upstairs), "prophesying" (divining) down from her usurped position – "false prophet". It is also interesting that her 'lofty' place was situated in the wall of the city. This indicates a breach in the city wall – a place of access for the enemy. Also, interesting that the eunuchs – those cut off from being fruitful – were serving her. Hmmm! Makes you think!

Another side thought here. Remember Elijah did not have authority to kill Ahab or to touch Jezebel. Just as David did not have authority to kill Saul – who was actually looking for David in order to kill him; as were Jezebel and Ahab with Elijah. The reason for this is to do with honour!

Both Elijah and David were honouring the position of their king. But, because Ahab was dead, Jezebel now became accessible.

But look at **verse 34** how, even though Jehu has Jezebel thrown down and drives over her, he still honours her position, "*she is after all a king's daughter*", and orders her remains be buried.

Holy Spirit, in all of this, showed me that when we are "cut off from being fruitful" – in other words, if we are not showing fruit in our ministry or are having a battle ministering effectively and everything seems a struggle, then we need to look to see what is hindering our ministry.

Jezebel gained entrance, through me playing Ahab to that spirit. That was just the beginning. I now needed to apply the right principle in order to deal with her.

Acknowledging my involvement, my lack of discernment and even my lack of knowledge or understanding, and repenting was the beginning freedom!

Chapter 8

So...have you played Ahab to a Jezebel spirit?

Have you given something, or someone, authority in your life by taking a line of least resistance?

Have you opened a door by walking incorrectly in the authority given you by the Lord?

Innocent enough questions, but ones we each need to ask ourselves because of the far-reaching implications. Especially if we are constantly being plagued by any one of these demonic forces, and are having the life sucked out of our ministries.

Are you portraying any of Ahab's characteristics?

Are you non-confrontational? - There are many out there who are just plain **confrontational** because they enjoy an argument. But, do you see problems and don't address them because you either don't want to deal with the "fall out", or are you hoping they will just go away?

Do you believe that you are invulnerable to Jezebel or her cohorts? In other words, do you believe that you have perfect discernment and are beyond being deceived? Believe me, that is deception itself! We are all fallible.

Do you like being in control? Are you "controlling"? Like having your own way? "My way or the highway!" Remember there is a huge difference between being an authoritative leader and being controlling. When you operate in true God given authority, the Holy Spirit will be in total control and you will know it – so will everyone else.

Do you micro-manage? This is a huge problem with people who are insecure because they will seem to delegate but then 'keep an eye' on what they've delegated. This shows a lack of faith in the persons you've delegated to and it also reveals pride. The pride might not be blatant but it is nevertheless visible.

Do you take the line of least resistance? Try to please everyone whether they are right or wrong? Scared of rocking the boat?

Are you unteachable? Something we would all like to believe we are not. But has anyone ever tried to bring correction to you, in any form? What has your response or reaction been? If you have refused to even consider that you might be wrong, then I believe you are showing signs of being unteachable. At least take it before the Lord!

One thing I have learned through the years about receiving correction or being challenged on a truth, is that if you keep your attitude humble and at least agree to take the situation before the Lord, He is then able to move on your behalf and will justify you if you are right. If not, He will certainly correct you!

Do you believe the "mantle" you wear; your position or calling; is about the position or the title? And do you believe that title brings with it a demand/command for respect? Remember respect is earned. The mantle you wear – in other words, your God-calling – is what sets you in position and gives you Godly authority. It is not the position or the title that make the man.

Remember God gives grace to the humble! (James 4:6)

Whatever "position" you think you have, if it doesn't "serve" then it is merely a title. If people recognise your God-given authority then they will automatically respect you. It's not because of who you are but because of who He is!

That little counsel was extra! Unfortunately, it is a subject sadly in need of teaching in the body of Christ.

Chapter 9

Freedom!

Remember there is a hierarchical chain or line of authority in the spirit. So, we need to look at where we have opened a door or where, more relevantly, we have begun to play "Ahab". Our insecurities, pride, selfishness and other flawed characteristics would be the open door to a Jezebel spirit. Where, in other words, have we "relegated", through our insecurities, authority to Jezebel and her cohorts.

**REMEMBER THERE IS A CHAIN OF HIERARCHY
AND AHAB IS THE BEGINNING!**

Firstly, we need to acknowledge that **we have personally** opened the doors to these spirits. This is not just an attack from the enemy. We have given these spirits **legal** right to be operating in our lives so, **we need to take responsibility**!

Then we need to recognise **how** and **where we've opened the doors** in order that we can then shut them, by repenting and cleansing ourselves.

Then, check what characteristics the spirit of Ahab portrays, **honestly and humbly measure yourself** against them and see what "measure of man (or woman)" you have allowed yourself to become. Our true measure is the Word of God, not those around us.

Repent of pride. Repent of selfish ambition. Repent of being unteachable, undiscerning, and generally believing you're impervious to deception. Holy Spirit will guide you and show you where you are at fault. It only takes

one insecurity to open the door!

Frustration, tiredness and not taking time to refresh ourselves in the Lord – spiritually as well as physically - are often areas which make us vulnerable.

Not taking Sabbath rest is a huge contributing factor. The Lord graciously taught me a huge lesson on this principle many years back.

I had just come off a 6-month ministry trip in the States and walked into a spiritual hornet's nest back home, so ran away. I ended up staying with a friend for a while. She had a house on the beach so I would walk up the beach each morning to have a "quiet time". This entailed praying in the spirit some and reading the odd scripture. Rather slapdash, I might add, because I was actually exhausted.

Well, one morning, I was quite a way up the beach when I heard an audible voice say "Will you shut up!" I stopped and looked around. I was totally alone, so carried on walking and kept 'praying in the spirit'. Well, the voice came again, "Will you shut up!" Still seeing no-one I assumed it must be the devil so rather irritatedly said, "Excuse me! I'm praying in the spirit!" Suddenly Holy Spirit spoke quite firmly from within me and said "No you're not, you're babbling!" I hit my knees fast! He then said "If you will not be quiet, how on earth will you hear what I need to tell you?" I repented and He then told me that for the next two weeks I needed to "lie down" – in other words "rest". He said "If you will not lie down, I will make you lie down!"

He did not have to explain the implications of disobeying, I KNEW!

Holy Spirit then explained that if I do not take regular Sabbath rest, He will require it **all** of me at some future time. So, if I haven't taken rest for a month because of ministry commitments, He would require 4 days (one day for each week) straight, in lieu of! He explained how essential those days of rest are for my wellbeing, spiritual as well as physical!

Sabbath is about rest. It's about having fun with family. It's about regrouping, catching your breath, letting go of the past week. It's about preparing yourself for the coming week by being at peace and allowing all

God's blessings and benefits to permeate you – spirit, soul and body!

Yet, most leaders, instead of resting, are either running around sorting things for Sunday service, or preparing sermons (a bit last minute don't you think!) or doing everything other than rest. We wonder then why the church is being served lukewarm meals, devoid of Holy Spirit and, therefore, why we see no growth! (Maturity, not numbers!)

Rest is actually a weapon. It's one of the strongest weapons against the enemy because it speaks of us being so secure in the Lord that we are able to rest in His presence whilst the battle rages around us. It's not a cop-out for doing nothing but is rather a faith statement in the spirit realm.

Waiting on God is as much of a weapon, and it's something we would be wise to do in these Sabbath rest times. This is a whole different teaching but the benefits are immense!

Isaiah 30:18 is one of my favourite scriptures and, which I believe speaks of the benefit of taking rest and waiting on the Father. (**AMP**) *And therefore the Lord earnestly waits, expecting, looking, and longing to be gracious to you; and, therefore He lifts Himself up, that He may have mercy on you and show loving kindness to you. For the Lord is a God of justice. Blessed, happy, fortunate, to be envied are all those who earnestly wait for Him, who expect and look and long for Him – **for His victory, His favour, His love, His peace, His joy and His matchless, unbroken companionship**!*

So, repent for not taking Sabbath rests and also for allowing yourself to become unfruitful – spiritually unproductive. The Lord is faithful and just to cleanse you of all unrighteousness and to restore you.

If we do not deal with the "Ahab" spirit in our lives we will never recognise when Jezebel is present. We need to expose where we have relegated authority or played Ahab to her before we can throw her down.

This is not something someone else can do for you – you need to do it yourself. If you have become a eunuch, one "cut off from being fruitful", then you need to throw that spirit down yourself. And it doesn't stop there! Don't forget her cohorts need to be dealt with as well.

Binding the Jezebel spirit, or trying to break its hold, will not remove this spirit from the picture. It is essential that you throw it down so it can be trampled underfoot. This means removing her from her 'lofty' position.

I didn't particularly want to acknowledge that I was a eunuch, but it was clear as day I had become one, so the onus was on me to throw this spirit of Jezebel down in order that she be put under Jesus feet.

This reminded me of Psalm 110:1 The Lord said to my Lord *"Sit in the place of honour at my right hand until I humble your enemies, making them a footstool under your feet"*.

Have a look again at the account of how Ahab came to his end. (Chapter 2 - **1 Kings 22:20-40**.)

I found it interesting that he was willing to let the Prophet Micaiah prophesy, but then tells him he's lying!

In verses **19 – 23** the Prophet even explains why Ahab would die in battle.
And Micaiah said, Hear the word of the Lord: I saw the Lord sitting on His throne, and all the host of heaven standing by Him on His right hand and on His left. And the Lord said, Who will entice Ahab to go up and fall at Ramoth-Gilead? One said this way, another said that way. Then came forth a spirit [of whom I am about to tell] and stood before the Lord and said, I will entice him. The Lord said to him, By what means? And he said, I will go forth and be a lying spirit in the mouths of all his prophets. [The Lord] said, You shall entice him and succeed also. Go forth and do it. So the Lord has put a lying spirit in the mouths of all these prophets; and the Lord has spoken evil concerning you.

Micaiah gets thrown in prison for this. Typical of an Ahab personality to blame the prophet rather than look for the fault in himself/herself!

What amazed me was, even having heard this word, Ahab still went into battle. God would deal with him!

The parallel the Lord showed me was the disdain which leadership, in the church at large, have for true Prophets, it will eventually lose them their ministries, as will divination.

Chapter 10

Divination Unwrapped

Remember, Jezebel does not work alone! Python and his cohorts, the Beguiling, Seducing and Controlling spirits all have their roles.

Ahab starts the process, Jezebel opens the door, and the cohorts do the work. Divination then becomes the ruling spirit in this whole bunch. So, not only does divination have to be dealt with but the spirits of control, beguilement and seduction as well.

Remember the picture of Mowgli, from Jungle Book, which I gave earlier? Ka uses seducing and beguiling to lure Mowgli into a false sense of security. His whole aim is to eat Mowgli!

The python spirit, or spirit of divination manifests itself by constricting ministry – suffocating the prophetic voice, **but it does not limit itself to the prophetic.** It will choke any vision and creativity. This spirit is territorial and does not want believers to take a city, region or nation.

So, once you've dealt with Ahab and Jezebel, it's then time to deal with Python. As I explained before, like any constrictor, this snake wraps itself around its prey. Therefore, dealing with him entails unwrapping him and shaking him off into the fire. Paul did that with a viper (**Acts 28**) and we have the authority to trample on snakes (**Psalm 91**).

It's not a simple matter with Python. Remember Python is associated with divination. So, let's have a look at what that constitutes.

Remember **Acts 16:16-18**? What the young slave girl was saying was the truth. Divination is so similar to a prophetic word that most people don't rightly discern it. It, simply put, is a word given in the wrong spirit or in the wrong timing. Its aim is to make the person feel good rather than bring glory to the Lord or draw the person closer to the Lord. In other words, it ministers to the soul – the mind the will or the intellect – rather than to the redeemed spirit of man.

A sad example is a woman I know who had a powerfully anointed teaching ministry. She began coveting other ministries because they seemed to get more attention, therefore more offerings. She was given a word, which I immediately discerned to be divination, about bigger ministry and all the things she had coveted. I pulled her aside later and told her that I had perceived the spirit of divination behind the word and that she needed to reject it. She refused – said that these were all things she desired and therefore it had to be God. Well, she got a home and then lost it. Got a more prominent ministry and then lost it and today is out of the ministry.

Then, some years back, I was at a 'gathering' where the gentleman ministering, a visiting speaker, did an altar call and was going to prophesy over those in the line. He came to an Asian lady and started by saying "My **son**, this is what the Lord would say". She stopped him and informed him she was a **lady**. He looked at her, almost rolled his eyes and continued – said again "my **son**, this is what the Lord would say". She stopped him three times and his final response to her was, "Well, whatever!" I was horrified to say the least and began binding the spirit of divination from operating.

Don't you think God knows whether or not the person in front of the prophet is male or female? The man's blatant lack of honour for the lady revealed the spirit behind the man. Had it been me standing in front of him I would have walked away, and maybe not as politely!

We have to remember that when we are speaking on behalf of God, we will be held responsible for those words.

Fortune tellers are also diviners. As are Psychics and Sorcerers (yes, they do still exist today and not just in Harry Potter movies!). What they tell people is demonically inspired rather than Holy Spirit truth. And, because they are attached to python – the spirit of divination – they will open the door to a spirit witchcraft which, in turn, brings a curse.

Rick Joyner said something in this regard which impacted me .... *"This is crucial for us to understand because there can be a thin line between the prophetic and sorcery. Sorcery is witchcraft, which Paul actually listed as one of the works of the flesh in Galatians. Witchcraft is counterfeit spiritual authority that seeks to use other spirits rather than the Holy Spirit. Witchcraft relies on patterns and formulas, and will always ultimately lead to manipulation, a control spirit, hype, or other carnal ways of using people rather than loving people and being used for the sake of people."*

Divination is initiated in the second heaven - Satan's domain - and is intended to bring the Church into disillusionment and discouragement. The more people receive revelation, albeit unwittingly, from the second heaven, the more hopelessness is released in their hearts. In reality, they are being deluded into seeking Satan's plans rather than God's. Unless the true prophetic ministry brings revelation from the third heaven - God's domain - from the presence of Father God, then this deception will prevail and hopelessness will bring heart sickness. Python then rules. With true revelation from the Father there is always hope of repentance, restoration and relationship with Him.

Whilst true prophecy, whether for edification, exhortation, correction or guidance, is intended to draw people closer to God, and His plans and purposes, divination will always focus on the person and their wants – either for acknowledgement and affirmation - or to delude them into seeking their own soulish desires rather than God's desires for them. This is what I call "entertainment prophecy". It tickles the ears of the hearer, appeals to their soul and makes them focus on things other than God.

Through divination the enemy will create discontent in the hearts of the people which will lead to discontent in their church, their families, their jobs – and so on. The reason being that divination will stifle, rather than produce, fruit and life. Whereas true prophecy should always produce fruit and life.

Unwrapping python means going back and reviewing 'prophetic' words you have received. Present them before the Father and hear which came from Him and which are based in your own soulish desires. Remember all prophecy (not the prophet) always needs to be judged.

We judge prophecy, not only according to the word, but according to what we already know from God in our hearts. Remember He always confirms His word by two or three witnesses.

Then, once you have dealt with Python, it's time to deal with his cohorts. You can bind them and you can break their hold and break their assignments. But I would encourage you to look for the principles within the Word to apply in order to displace those principalities as well.

The reason we apply a principle to displace a principality, is to ensure the place the principality has vacated is filled with the word and therefore no longer vulnerable to the enemy.

Chapter 11

Principles

In my earlier studies of Elijah, I was always amazed that he never dealt with Jezebel. Even when she wrote him the "dear John" – or rather "Elijah, I'm going to kill you!" letter - he ran from her rather than confronting her. I remember, as a very young Christian, asking the Lord about this.

Elijah was the prophet who called down fire, which burned the companies of soldiers sent to find him. He had closed the heavens so it didn't rain for three and a half years. He was fed by ravens. He had raised a child from the dead. He had rebuilt the altar at Mt Carmel. He had killed over 400 Baal prophets, opened the heavens for rain again and then had run ahead of Ahab's chariot to Jezreel. My question to the Father was "Why – with all this power and authority – was he not able to take down Jezebel?"

The Lord's response was to teach me a few truths.

Firstly, to always honour leaders – no matter how good or bad! Ahab was the king and Elijah's dealings had to be through the king. Jezebel was firstly Ahab's, then ultimately God's, responsibility, not Elijah's. You will also note that the Lord did not grant Elijah permission to take Ahab out either! Just as David was not allowed to kill Saul, but honoured him until he was eventually killed in battle.

Remember to always separate the sin from the sinner! God loves the sinner but hates the sin. We need to as well!

When we dishonour leaders, we open ourselves to attack. God will use the Spirit of God – the Holy Spirit - in you to convict those in error, and this will, more often than not, cause a backlash. The enemy does not like being exposed! So, walk in love!

Secondly, the Lord taught me not to allow myself to get so tired that I wouldn't have the strength to deal with the backlash of the enemy. He said it is essential I take time for myself – to recoup my strength, spiritual as well as physical, especially after a time of ministry. He said too that, when we've had our biggest victories, we become extremely vulnerable to the backlash of the enemy.

Then, when we are in a place of transition, especially in ministry, we also become particularly vulnerable. The enemy is looking to gain entry, in order to cause us to exalt his lies over the promises of God. "I'm the only one doing anything. Everyone is attacking or conspiring against me. The people aren't really interested in what I have to say – they all want to kill me". Elijah said pretty much all of that. (**1Kings 19:10**)

The enemy used all these lies to "cut Elijah off from being fruitful". It took Angels to minister strength to him, but it also took for Elijah to begin the long journey back to where He could focus on the still small voice of the Lord and recognise that his work was not yet done. Praise God he did!

Deliverance

A wonderful precept I learned some years ago is something I referred to earlier. **To displace a principality, you need to apply a principle.** This precept applies in every part of the demonic realm, not just for the removal of Ahab, Jezebel and her cohorts!

If you want to be free and remain free of these demonic influences, principalities and powers, or rulers of darkness, you need to apply Biblical principles or truths to the areas where the enemy has rule. The more time you spend in the word; the more time you walk in the fruit of the Spirit; and the more you allow God's spiritual endowments – His gifts – to operate in and through you, the more you will walk in freedom. Humility, pain and suffering will truly become strength, grace and glory.

Because of the times we live in, many are geared to "instant" this and "fast" that, which unfortunately seems to pertain to the spiritual life of many as well. They want a quick fix rather than to deal with the continuous battle, which is the truth of our walk with the Lord. It is not an easy walk – Jesus Himself said, in this world we would have persecution because of Him. He also said the path was narrow. Then He said *"And he who does not take up his cross and follow Me [cleave steadfastly to Me, conforming wholly to My example in living and, if need be, in dying also] is not worthy of Me."* (**Matt 10:38**)

TO DISPLACE A PRINCIPALITY, YOU HAVE TO APPLY A PRINCIPLE!

So, quit looking for methodology or a quick fix and begin applying the principles of the Word to displace the principalities in your life. To do so, you need to understand which principle to use. That is why we have a manual called The Bible! For the Truth to set you free, you need to KNOW the Truth!

The precept behind applying principles to displace principalities, is to ensure that, where you have dealt with the enemy and have 'expelled' him from your life, you not only clean up your act but, you fill those areas the enemy has vacated with the Word of God.

Luke 11:24 - 26 *When the unclean spirit has gone out of a person, it roams through waterless (dry) places in search of a place of rest; and finding none it says, I will go back to my house from which I came and when it arrives, it finds the place swept and put in order and furnished and decorated. And it goes and brings other spirits, seven of them, more evil that itself, and they enter in, settle down, and dwell there; and the last state of that person is worse than the first.*

This is such an important scripture to remember and apply!

Another key area, the Lord has brought to my attention recently, has to do with the Helmet of Salvation. Yes, it's part of the armour of God.

We all claim to have on the full armour of God but, frankly, if we did, we wouldn't have the problems we do have in dealing with the enemy.

Ephesians 6:10,11(AMP) *In conclusion, be strong in the Lord [be empowered through your union with Him]; draw your strength from Him [that strength which His boundless might provides]. Put on the whole armour [the armour of a heavy-armed soldier which God supplies], that you may be able successfully to stand up against [all] the strategies and deceits of the devil.* (Underline mine)

God's armour is impenetrable!

He also said in **Isaiah 54:17** *But no weapon that is formed against you shall prosper, and every tongue that shall rise against you in judgement you shall show to be in the wrong. This [peace, righteousness, security, triumph over opposition] is the heritage of the servants of the Lord [those in whom the ideal Servant of the Lord is reproduced]*

Chapter 12

The Helmet

The Lord showed me that many in the Body have removed their helmet of salvation (**Ephesians 6:17**) because it has become too "hot". God's helmet not only protects but it also convicts!

Several books have been written on the battleground being the mind. Yet if we wore our helmets the enemy would not be able to take the pot-shots at our minds, which he does. In other words – when our minds are uncovered the enemy has access! Simple fact. The helmet covers the mind – which is where our conscience is - it is also the safeguard against the onslaught of the enemy on our minds.

So, what does the helmet of salvation entail and how have we become exposed?

If we break down the Hebrew (*kowba or qowba*) and Greek (*perikephalaia*) words for 'helmet', we will have a picture of something which has the domed shape of the head and totally encompasses or surrounds the mind. In other words, it covers the whole head and seizes or embraces the attention – the conscious mind.

So, if this helmet is called the Helmet of Salvation, then it obviously refers to our salvation. Because of this, we need to truly understand salvation.

In the Old Testament there are basically three different words for salvation, the New Testament has two - but they all mean the same – **deliverance, help, safety, victory, liberty, prosperity, welfare and health**. WOW!

In other words, the helmet of salvation is our assurance of God's provision for; our deliverance, our victory, His help, our safety, our liberty (freedom), our prosperity, welfare and health.

So, every time the enemy comes with something opposite, with which to bombard our minds, the helmet of salvation's response to the attack is assurance that we have been delivered; we are victorious; God is a very present help in times of trouble; we are safe in Him; we are free in Him; whom the Son sets free is free indeed!; we are prosperous; we do fare well; we are blessed, and we walk in divine health. Truly, what more could we ask for!

It begs the question then – if we are walking in defeat and are battling in these areas which salvation promises, does this mean that we are no longer saved? Emphatically NO! All it means is that we have removed our helmet, our assurance; our protection, somewhere along the way.

But before you start beating yourself up, let's go back to Elijah and take a leaf from his book once again.

Let's look at **1 Kings 19**

Elijah runs from Jezebel and ends up in the wilderness. The Lord sends Angels to minister to him and tells him to go down to Mt Horeb (Mt Sinai) where he ends up in the back of a cave.

He is still not in the spiritual place God wants him, which we can tell by the question God asks. Elijah is battling the effects of dealing with the first two spirits – Ahab and Jezebel. The Lord asks him twice, *"Elijah, what are you doing here?"* and both times his response is the same, *"I have been very jealous for the Lord God of Hosts, because the Israelites have forsaken Your covenant, thrown down Your altars, and slain Your prophets with the sword. And I, I only, am left, and they seek my life to destroy it"*. One translation says *"All of Israel want to kill me!"*

This seems like a valid response until you read the preceding chapters. Elijah, however, still can't see past what he thinks is his personal failure. The enemy bombards his mind with every thought which is contrary to the word of God concerning him or the actual facts.

Only Jezebel is seeking his life. He had just restored God's altars and brought the people back to the Lord. He had killed the Baal prophets. God's track record in his life was huge, but all of that went by the board because he had forgotten **Whose** and **who** he was!

God calls Elijah to the front of the cave and begins demonstrating His power to him. He shows Elijah that He is not in the wind or the earthquake or the fire, but rather in the still small voice within. In other words – *it's not by might, nor by power, but by My Spirit, says the Lord!* **(Zechariah 4:6)**

Elijah then does something prophetic which I have applied several times in my own life since "seeing" it. He takes his mantle – which represents his calling, his office as prophet, all that God has declared he is – and wraps it round his head. He applies God's word; God's calling; God's commissioning; God's provision – his "helmet of salvation" – to the place where he is fighting his greatest battle, the mind! He has to shut the enemy's voice out of his head – the self-doubt, the recriminations, the lies – by applying what God has declared about him, in order to once again hear that still small voice within him.

It was only once Elijah had stilled the voice of the enemy in his head that God was able to speak to his heart and re-commission him.

Do you see how this relates?

Some of you reading this will be thinking your ministry is over and that you've missed the mark so big that, like Elijah, you are wanting the Lord just to take you home. Like Elijah, you are saying *"I've had enough Lord. Take my life, for I am no better than my ancestors who have already died"* (**1 Kings 19:4**)

I have always maintained that the enemy overplays his hand, especially when we have experienced spiritual breakthrough or victory. He attacks and exposes what God is wanting healed in us. We don't recognise it though because we allow ourselves to become blind-sided and forget who we are in Christ.

If you remember, I mentioned earlier that I had applied the same principle Elijah had - when he prophetically covered his head with his mantle to shut out the voice of the enemy, in order for him to hear the still small voice of the Spirit within.

The following is a personal testimony of how this works in reality.

The Lord had launched me into ministry in the States back in 1995. I was in my first year there and still trying to understand all that ministry entailed.

One evening, at the beginning of a long holiday weekend, the Lord told me to take out all the prophetic words He had spoken over me – either directly, or through His prophets - and to begin to encourage myself with these words. I've always kept a folder with these words, so began to read them and declare out loud who God says I am and what He has called and commissioned me to do. In other words, I wrapped my 'mantle' around my head. This took a few hours. I had no idea at the time how God was preparing me for the attack which was to come.

No sooner had I gone through my prophetic words than I began to travail. I had no idea why, or what it was about, but wept out of the depths of my spirit. For the rest of the weekend I wept and prayed in the spirit. I couldn't eat, I couldn't sleep – I was a wreck and had no idea what I was battling. BUT I held on to the words the Lord had had me encourage myself with. I knew who I was and what God had called me to and I was secure in Him because of it.

On the Monday afternoon I finally discovered the attack had come through a false accusation spoken to a friend, and others, concerning me. The accusation, was everything contra to what I knew God had said about me and what He had called me to.

Because of where I was spiritually – strong and covered in the Lord – my response was "*Is this what this is all about – false accusation? Lord, I choose **not** to be offended, **not** to react, but to forgive and to release*". Immediately peace came and the storm was over for me. I won't say the attack was over, but it was no longer **my** battle. I walked in total peace in this situation.

I also learned a very valuable lesson, about not taking offense, at that time. You see, when we "take" offense, we "own" it. And, because we "own" it, we carry a spirit of strife with us wherever we go. It affects our ministry and every other area of our lives. But when we choose **not** to take offense – **not** to be offended – we no longer own it but the person who caused the offense does, and it will affect them the same way.

So, please, put on your 'helmet'! Repent for having removed it or for not understanding and valuing its significance! When it feels 'hot', ask Holy Spirit to show you why He's convicting you and what you need to change. Keep it on, so the enemy will not be able to take the 'pot shots' at your mind, which he so enjoys doing!

Remember too, there is a difference between conviction and condemnation. Conviction is when Holy Spirit wants to correct something in your life or pull you back on course if you are straying. He will always give you victory and a way out of the situation - most likely through repentance. Condemnation, however, comes from the enemy to break you down and to pull you out of alignment with the Lord. It is full of damnation which is from the pits of hell.

Deliverance is a subject seldom taught anymore in the church today, but it is one which we had better begin paying attention to or we will not win the battle ahead. It is too big a subject to be dealt with in this writing, but there are many excellent books out there.

Chapter 13

Testimony Time

The following testimonies will give you some idea of how Jezebel gains access through an Ahab personality.

The Pastor of a church I attended many years ago was a precious man of God – powerful foundational teacher. But he made a statement from the pulpit one day which signalled, I believe, the downfall of his ministry and the eventual break up of that church. He said *"You may be able to pull the wool over my eyes, but you will never pull the wool over my wife's eyes!"* In my heart I literally groaned. I knew he and his wife were personally going to be challenged by this statement, and that the church would enter a time of real warfare. There was no teaching about Ahab, Jezebel or any of her cohorts at the time, so we had very little in our arsenal with which to take on the enemy with.

Being a fairly new convert and very new to the prophetic, I wasn't always sure what I was discerning or hearing, so it was difficult to speak to anyone about this initially. I just prayed in the spirit. A few days later I shared it with my two intercessor friends and they agreed that there was a battle about to begin.

As new Christians we didn't have the knowledge of spiritual warfare we do now, so we did what we knew to do – asked the Lord to intervene. Two of us were counsellors so were part of the ministry team. Not two weeks later it was as though all hell was loosed against the church and against us personally. Much happened during the following couple of months but I want to highlight a few areas in order to point out the error.

The pastor's wife began falsely accusing innocent people of causing strife. She publicly made statements about people which were totally unfounded and untrue. No amount of trying to talk to her would get through. She was absolutely resolute and irrational in her decisions and her accusations, and the pastor backed her without question.

A fellow (female) counsellor was "seen", by the pastor's wife, praying with the head counsellor (male) in the prayer room and the pastor's wife accused her of having an affair with this man. Actually, she was the only one accused and told to step down from ministry. The male head counsellor wasn't even aware of the situation – he only found out after we had left that ministry.

At the same time I was approached by the pastor himself to become his personal intercessor. I refused on the grounds that I was a young single woman. He had informed me that he would require me to spend many hours alone with him, something I thought totally unwise – especially in the light of what my fellow counsellor had just been accused of. He became angry, accused me of being in rebellion and basically commanded me to do as he said. I refused, so was told to step down from my position as counsellor and intercessor as well.

A few of us spoke, separately, to the elders about this and the several other instances which had arisen with others on the ministry team, and they advised us not to discuss it amongst ourselves but just to pray, so we did. They then approached the pastor and spoke to him but he still refused to acknowledge that he and his wife were in the wrong. We were once again accused of causing strife.

There were several other nasty incidents which don't bear exposing but, suffice it to say, God very quickly released us from the ministry and led us to another where we were able to grow in safety.

It was a simple statement the pastor had made, but one made in pride. Immediately the enemy came to challenge it. I believe God allowed it to expose the deception. None of us are above being deceived. We have to exercise discernment all the time and be humble enough to admit where we might have missed it.

After we left the congregation diminished somewhat over the next year or so and eventually the pastor and his wife left. It was really hard on everyone involved, many were hurt and it took a while for healing to come. Especially because the Lord had used this ministry to introduce revival to the city. We had seen untold miracles through this work. All ceased.

In the light of what we now know about the Ahab, Jezebel and Python spirits, briefly, this how they worked in this situation.

Firstly, the pastor believing his wife was above deception, was deception in itself. By his statement from the pulpit he gave authority to a Jezebel spirit which ultimately opened the door to the spirit of divination, Python, who eventually squeezed the life out of the church.

The enemy effectively used divination to shut down a potentially powerful ministry. God had done some amazing miracles in and through this ministry. The growth had been astounding. We had gone from about 20 people in the pastor's lounge to a congregation of around 350 in about three months. We saw miracles almost on a daily basis. The pastor was one of the best foundational teachers I have met. He put a truly solid foundation of the word in all of us, one which has stood me in good stead through the years. Sad!

REMEMBER, DIVINATION IS A RIGHT WORD GIVEN IN THE WRONG SPIRIT.

The following case is someone well known to me so, for their protection, I have purposefully not revealed the identities of those involved. Remember this book is about exposing spiritual personalities and not human individuals! This is not about exposing people but exposing the spirits who control them.

Some years back I counselled a fellow prophet who had been playing

"Ahab" to a Jezebel spirit. This nearly shut down their ministry and took several years for he and his wife to break free.

This is their testimony. "By the time we discovered what was going on – we were totally blindsided – it took every bit of faith we had, as well as a lot of counsel, deliverance and prayer, to break free.

We were in a situation where we did not immediately recognise what spirits were controlling our worship leader. The anointing on him for worship, or so I thought, was truly great. We realised he had several problems though and, in our own wisdom and strength, thought we would be able to counsel him through these, and/or even pray for his deliverance. We had a few conversations about some of his issues but nothing ever seemed to change. Not for long anyway. Because of his ability to lead worship we tried ignoring the problem. We did not hear God at all in the situation, till it was almost too late.

Ministry was taking off in a big way and we were so busy that there wasn't time to deal with his issues in any significant way so, we took the line of least resistance for as long as we could. When the situation got unbearably bad, we would take authority and see a little change for a short time before it would rear its head again.

We began noticing a pattern. Just before any special ministry programme, he would start doing things, like picking arguments, or accusing myself or others of things which were totally unfounded. This would steal my focus and, get me so riled, it would take all my time to calm down enough to be able to hear the Lord and to minister effectively.

Then we found the prophetic was drying up. We knew God was wanting to speak to us and could hear Him clearly but the prophetic was still not flowing the way it had in the past. We found ourselves warring in the spirit all the time - which became a distraction in itself, because we didn't know what we were fighting. Little things which we thought were just strange idiosyncrasies with this person turned out to be huge issues, which we still presumptuously thought we had authority over. Mostly, we felt that if we just ignored it, it would go away – that he would stop hassling us if we didn't give him a platform by reacting.

By not taking authority over that spirit right in the beginning, and confronting what I was seeing operating through this person, I was clearly playing "Ahab" to a Jezebel spirit. Because of that line of least resistance, I had allowed the spirit of Divination onto the scene as well. I was being slowly squeezed to death spiritually and so was our ministry.

God made it perfectly and plainly clear we needed to part company. It was difficult and pretty acrimonious, but we parted ways.

Then we realised, even though this person was no longer part of the ministry, we were still having the same problem. The prophetic was still not moving the way it had originally and other issues began arising. We spent much time praying and eventually the Lord led us to a few very significant books on Jezebel and the Python spirit.

Our knowledge grew but we still weren't seeing the breakthrough. Altar ministry seemed to be becoming less and less. We took authority and rebuked and did all that we knew to do but we weren't experiencing the freedom in the Spirit we knew we should.

In desperation I phoned a fellow prophet and asked her for counsel, to see what it was blocking us in the spirit. After some prayer she identified the spirit of Python. We had dealt with Jezebel by this time but the "constrictor", Python, was still there and quietly squeezing the life out of my wife and I and also the ministry. When we understood the dynamics between Ahab, Jezebel and Divination, we realised that, until we stopped 'tolerating' the spirits of Jezebel and Divination, our ministry would not move forward. Once revelation came it was easy to expose, rebuke and get free.

The biggest challenge since then has been to constantly be aware of any Ahab characteristics we might have the tendency to display and which would have the potential to open the doors again for Jezebel and her cohorts to have place in our lives and ministry again".

AHAB CHARACTERISTICS HAVE THE POTENTIAL TO OPEN THE DOOR TO JEZEBEL

It was taking the line of least resistance, by not openly confronting **the spirit** (not the person), which allowed deception to come into this man's ministry. The presumption of thinking they could handle the situation, without first consulting the Lord, was the first mistake.

We have to be extremely careful who we are linked with in ministry. There is natural talent and then there is anointing from God. It is essential we discern the difference. Not everyone who says "I am the Christ", or "I am the anointed of God" is from Him. **Matthew 24** tells us many will be deceived and I believe it's because we often exhibit the characteristics of Ahab that we open ourselves for this kind of deception.

Let's look at the two examples of deception here.

In the first testimony, it was the Pastor's belief that his wife could do no wrong. As she stood as co-pastor with him (and please don't let this make you exclude your spouses from ministry – this could have been anyone!!), he relegated authority to her. If he, instead, had remarked that his wife was *'less inclined to be duped because she was more discerning than him'*, we might have had a different outcome. But his emphatic statement, believing that she was beyond deception, is what nailed it. For some reason he seemed to think she was spiritually superior to him – big mistake! We all have the same Holy Spirit and no one person is 'greater' than another!

When I refused to be his personal intercessor, the Pastor took it as a personal affront. He was oblivious to the implications involved. It could have been someone else more vulnerable than me. Personal intercessors – if they are required to spend much time alone with the pastor, as he expected me to, in my opinion, should be same gender. This avoids "the appearance of evil".

Especially because it is such an intimate ministry.

Then, instead of the Pastor listening to those who had been falsely accused, hearing both sides of the story, and praying into the situation, he refused to get involved. He *assumed* that his wife was doing the right thing so let her get on with it. He did not even speak to those who had been falsely accused, to verify his wife's claims, he relegated the authority to her and she alone dealt with them.

Even when the elders approached him, he still stood firm. He took the correction as a personal attack. This opened him to more deception.

Remember, always, that you are dealing with spirits and these spirits are not gender specific so could attach to either male or female!

REMEMBER GOD LOVES THE SINNER AND HATES THE SIN, SO SEPARATE THE SIN FROM THE SINNER ALWAYS!

In the second testimony, my friend did not confront the Jezebel spirit either. He wrongly assumed an unrighteous authority, by his belief that he could handle the worship leader's problems without consulting God. Had he been discerning, from the beginning, he would have recognised the difference between anointing and talent, which is especially important when choosing a worship leader! Then, by allowing himself to become distracted, he missed the warning signs Holy Spirit was alerting him to. When the person manifested in the way he did, prior to ministry times, taking the line of least resistance opened the door even further.

So, Ahab, in both instances, was beguiled, seduced and manipulated by Jezebel as he relegated authority to her. He acted presumptuously. She and her cohorts legally moved in. In the first instance the pastor and his wife left the ministry, and the second took some knocks but is up and running well again. Praise God!

None of this happened overnight. It took a year or so from when the situation arose in the first scenario before the pastor left but many were caught in the aftermath of that destruction.

The repercussions are always far reaching and affect so many people.

Chapter 14

The Cleansing

Before you begin, remember **Luke 11:24-29**. Be sure to fill the house you have cleansed, lest the enemy comes back with more of his friends to occupy once again!

To be rid of Ahab will require repentance. If you can identify with one or more of the characteristics an Ahab spirit portrays, or have the slightest inkling, that you might be portraying one or more characteristic, then it's time to repent. Ask the Lord to forgive you for your participation in Ahab's rule in your life, and in your ministry. Especially if you are a leader!

Repent for having disdained or ignored the prophetic and, more specifically, God's true prophets. Repent for having 'married' or tolerated Jezebel. Repent for having given her authority in your life and in your church. Repent for pride, arrogance and any other of the characteristics you might portray. Quite frankly, it would be wise to repent of all of them! If you need reminding there is a list at the end of the book which will help you.

Then, because you have been cut off from being fruitful – serving Jezebel – repent and ask the Lord's forgiveness for having put aside discernment and the gifts of the spirit in order to serve her. Repent for having exalted her above your giftings, callings and the truth of who you are in Christ.

Remember **Romans 11:29** *For God's gifts and His call are irrevocable. [He never withdraws them when once they are given, and He does not change His mind about those to whom He gives His grace or to whom He sends His call.]*

Thank the Lord for His promises, appropriate them once again and allow restoration to begin.

Next, that Jezebel spirit needs to be thrown down! Once Ahab is dealt with and she no longer has authority, or a right to be there, she will be exposed. It is then that Jehu can come on the scene and trample her in the city gates. Break her hold. Throw her down from the high place she has occupied in your life and ministry and put her under Jesus feet!

Then it's time to deal with Divination (Python). We unwrap divination by repenting of receiving, or entertaining, any word that is not of God. Any prophetic word or teaching which does not come from the throne of God must be rejected. Get rid of them! Do not just throw them on a shelf somewhere! Throw them on the fire! Shake off that snake of renown into the fire and shut the door!

Repent for a lack of discernment.

Repent for having taken off your helmet of salvation.

Repent for allowing yourself to be beguiled, seduced and controlled by any one of these demonic forces. Bind them from operating in your life and ministry, then command them to leave, in Jesus Name.

Apply the word!

Matthew 16:19 *I will give you the keys of the kingdom of Heaven; and whatever you bind (declare to be improper and unlawful) on earth must be what is already bound in heaven; and whatever you loose (declare lawful) on earth must be what is already loosed in heaven.*

Psalm 51 (AMP) has always been a favourite because it is such a beautiful 'repentance' prayer. Pray it over yourself.

Have mercy upon me, O God, according to Your steadfast love; according to the multitude of Your tender mercy and loving-kindness blot out my transgressions.

Wash me thoroughly [and repeatedly] from my iniquity and guilt and cleanse and make me wholly pure from my sin!

For I am conscious of my transgressions and I acknowledge them; my sin is ever before me.

Against You, You only, have I sinned and done that which is evil in Your sight, so that You are justified in Your sentence and faultless in Your judgement.

Behold You desire truth in the inner being; make me therefore to know wisdom in my inmost heart.

Purify me with hyssop, and I shall be clean; wash me, and I shall [in reality] be whiter than snow.

Make me to hear joy and gladness and be satisfied; let the bones which You have broken rejoice.

Hide Your face from my sins and blot out all my guilt and iniquities.

Create in me a clean heart, O God, and renew a right, persevering and steadfast spirit within me.

Cast me not away from Your presence and take not Your Holy Spirit from me.

Restore to me the joy of Your salvation and uphold me with a willing spirit.

Then I will teach transgressors Your ways, and sinners shall be converted and return to You.

Deliver me from bloodguiltiness and death, O God, the God of my salvation, and my tongue shall sing aloud of Your righteousness (Your rightness and Your justice).

O Lord, open my lips, and my mouth shall show forth Your praise.

For you delight not in sacrifice, or else would I give it; You find no pleasure in burnt offering.

My sacrifice [the sacrifice acceptable] to God is a broken spirit; a broken and contrite heart [broken down with sorrow for sin and humbly and thoroughly penitent], such, O God, You will not despise.

It is always good to pray the Word. There are a few other scriptures which you can use and I suggest you go and dig for them, and more, yourself.

Remember **Proverbs 25:2** says *It is the glory of God to conceal a thing, but the glory of kings is to search out a thing.*

Once you have repented, I suggest you spend some time in worship and take Communion to seal your deliverance. This always will bring you into the presence of the Father. Then ask Holy Spirit to fill you afresh and anew.

Holy Spirit of God, I ask that You fill me. Fill, to overflowing, every area where the enemy has been evicted and banished from my life. Fill me, spirit, soul and body, with Your truth and Your light.

Remember to fill and keep filling the places the enemy has vacated – lest he come back with all his buddies! STAY IN THE WORD!

Paul prays in **Ephesians 1:17** – that *the God of our Lord Jesus Christ may grant you a spirit of wisdom and revelation [of insight into the mysteries and secrets] in the [deep and intimate] knowledge of Him.*

Proverbs 4, is packed with wisdom, well worth meditating on. Verse **7b** is a powerful 'nugget'. *And with all you have gotten,* ***get understanding (discernment, comprehension, and interpretation).***

Chapter 15

The Walk

I'm not saying it's going to be easy. It never is and anyone who says it is, is lying! BUT God!

Once you have fully dealt with Ahab, Jezebel, Python (divination) and all their cohorts, get filled and stay filled with Holy Spirit, then remain in the word. Call for understanding. Appropriate the gift of discernment – unpack all it entails – get full understanding. Allow Holy Spirit to place a guard over your heart and mind, and keep your helmet of salvation on. Repent for having taken it off in the first place! Then allow that which Christ paid for at Calvary to dissolve all the doubts and fears and questions the enemy has bombarded your mind with. Let the Word of God answer his lies.

Jesus Himself applied principle to displace the principality when he was tempted in the wilderness. Each time he was tested or tempted, He responded, "*It is written*". Let this be our response too.

When your helmet becomes too "hot"; when you are being convicted by the Word of God or by what Holy Spirit is revealing; when you've exalted the lies of the enemy over the promises of God - learn to repent quickly. Rather than removing, or ignoring, that which is convicting you, repent and get right before God!

Paul talks of us searing our conscience. When we do, it removes the protection of our salvation.

So, if you want to get rid of the enemy in your life, begin to apply the principles which will displace him.

"Put on every piece of God's armour so you will be able to resist the enemy in the time of evil. Then after the battle you will be standing firm. Stand your ground, putting on the belt of truth and the body armour of God's righteousness. For shoes, put on the peace that comes from the Good News so that you will be fully prepared. In addition to all of these, hold up the shield of faith to stop the fiery arrows of the devil. Put on salvation as your helmet, and take the sword of the Spirit which is the Word of God. Pray in the Spirit at all times and on every occasion. Stay alert and be persistent in your prayers for all believers everywhere". ***(Ephesians 6:11 – 18)***

Let us be done with playing Ahab to that Jezebel spirit! Let us refuse to give her authority in our lives. Let us be done with divination! Let us come out of darkness and be ones who walk into the light, which gets brighter and brighter as unto the noonday sun!

God bless you as you walk out your salvation!

Chapter 16
The Wrap Up

As I said in the prologue, divination is rife in the world. Every false prophet's voice seems louder than those who are genuinely commissioned by God. It's time for the true prophets to come out of the cave! We need the true word of God to be released in the earth.

The Hebrew year 5780 (2020 in the Gregorian calendar) – represented by the Hebrew letter *Peh* which speaks of the 'breath' – also began a New Era. So, we shouldn't be surprised the enemy is doing everything in his power to cut off the breath or pervert it through false (fake) words as much as he can. It's time for the *ekklesia* (God's called-out ones) to take a stand!

When I began studying Elijah's story some years back, the subject of another book, I came across the passage where he encounters Ahab's servant, Obadiah. Obadiah was the governor of Ahab's house. He was obviously a believer because, when Jezebel went on a killing spree of God's prophets, Obadiah was the one who hid the prophets in a cave.

What was interesting was Obadiah's name, it means, *Serving Jah*. His name comes from two root words – *bond servant or, to serve,* and – *the Lord most vehement* – which is the same as *Jehovah*.

I believe Obadiah represents the Apostolic, which is **supposed** to 'govern' Ahab's household, which I believe represents the church. In other words, **the Apostolic must have a ruling position in order to keep the Prophets safe**. Unfortunately, because Ahab has relegated authority to Jezebel, the Prophets have had to be hidden.

But it's time!

Would the true Apostles and Prophets please take their place! Would the true church please stand up!

It's time to rule and reign!

Characteristics List for easy Reference

Ahab
Arrogant
Insecure
Petulant
Martyr complex
Easily manipulated
Takes line of least resistance
Relegates authority – doesn't delegate
Micro-manages
Doesn't handle conflict well
Whiner
Greedy
Sullen
Sulks if doesn't get own way
Lacks discernment
Seldom practices what he preaches
Obedient only when it suits
Unteachable
Justifier
False pride of position
Compromiser
A fence-sitter

Jezebel
Arrogant
Controlling
Won't listen to reason – unless it's to his/her advantage
Encourages false prophets
Seductive
Wilful
Headstrong
Feels entitled

Unteachable
Promotes witchcraft
Manipulative
Dominating

Python
Constrictor
Suffocates victim – cuts off the breath
Shuts up the true prophets
Stealthy
False prophet
Beguiles
Lulls into false sense of security
Deceiver
Liar
Anti-Christ
Controlling